BRIDGE PASSAGES

BRIDGE PASSAGES

George Szirtes

For Paul and Sandor
with best wishes.
George Szirtes 92

Oxford New York
OXFORD UNIVERSITY PRESS
1991

Oxford University Press, Walton Street, Oxford OX2 6DP
Oxford New York Toronto
Delhi Bombay Calcutta Madras Karachi
Petaling Jaya Singapore Hong Kong Tokyo
Nairobi Dar es Salaam Cape Town
Melbourne Auckland
and associated companies in
Berlin Ibadan

Oxford is a trade mark of Oxford University Press

First published in Oxford Poets
as an Oxford University Press paperback 1991

British Library Cataloguing in Publication Data
Szirtes, George, 1948–
Bridge passages
I. Title
821.914
ISBN 0–19–282821–5

Library of Congress Cataloging in Publication Data
Szirtes, George, 1948–
Bridge passages/George Szirtes.
p. cm.—(Oxford poets)
I. Title II. Series.
PR6069.Z7B75 1991 821'.914–dc20
ISBN 0–19–282821–5

Typeset by Wyvern Typesetting Ltd.
Printed in Hong Kong

For my friends in Hungary

ACKNOWLEDGEMENTS

ACKNOWLEDGEMENTS are due to the following publications where some of these poems first appeared: *Encounter*, *First and Always* (Faber), *Illuminations*, *Lines Review*, *The Listener*, *New Hungarian Quarterly*, *The Observer*, *Owl*, *Poetry Book Society Anthology 1988–89* and *1989–90*, *Poetry Review*, *The Spectator*, *The Rialto*, *The Times Literary Supplement*, *ZLR* and BBC's *Poetry Now*.

The translations from Ottó Orbán appear in 'The Blood of the Walsungs' (Corvina Press, 1991).

I would also like to thank the British Council whose generosity enabled me to spend the eight months from January to August 1989 in Budapest.

CONTENTS

NIGHT FERRY

And our idea of hell is the night ferry.
A deep slow swell, the purser in his booth,
A thumping head no aspirin can soothe
And two or three lads quietly getting merry.

It's normal, that is all, the bottom line
Of nightmare, meaning nothing, emptiness
Which finds us though we leave it no address
And leaves a pain that art cannot refine.

It's almost three o'clock. The vessel rolls:
We draw our coats about us. The idea
Of sea enters our minds and washes clear
The bodies by their sinks and toilet bowls.

RECORDING

A distant night train and a dog. Then crickets.
And fingers turning the leaves of a book.
Insects hover at the window. The hedges lean back.
Their curving arms are paths of rockets.

The final sensations are necessarily fragmentary,
like voices on a tape recorder repeating . . .
and there's the horror. Somebody goes on quoting
fragments, unattributable, without memory.

BRIDGE PASSAGES I

DRAWING THE CURTAIN

'Observe the convolutions of this frieze.'
The voice comes to me like a tourist guide
explaining the explicable.
To slide your hand behind the stucco, seize
the mortar and move gently round inside
makes sensuous and tangible.

Curved galleries like zips, a moral fall
of stairs and liftshafts, and the flickering
inconsequentiality
of every human movement—material
and light—make an expanding, shapeless ring
of meaning and capacity.

An accident defines what breaks the heart—
the history of architecture, not of form
but aberration, lapse of taste,
the way an elevation tears apart
its brick integument before the storm
that lays the human pattern waste.

It is quite possible to love a face
the moment it appears and then is lost
in the darkness within windows, shut
within the belly of the commonplace,
that achieves the equivocation of a ghost
or a telephone with wires cut.

It turns to radios barely heard, until
the loud convergence of external moments
threatening familiar sound,
when history packs her bags and pays the bill
long owing, and the intimate events,
the lives of chairs and beds, are drowned.

Compulsive patterns of crude ironwork
in the glass panel of a door, the dangerous
geometry of aerials
on roofs the colour of air, and every quirk,
irregularity, each hint of madness,
are her discarded materials.

The miracles of value, allegiance, loss
are hardly different from a moving curtain.
A hand appears and a shape holds
a single space before they're drawn across,
and in that movement everything uncertain
hurts and gathers in the folds.

A DOMESTIC FAUST

Now come into the room. Turn on the light.
It's almost evening. Make yourself a drink.
The hiss of gas and the faint lisp
of match on sandpaper, the sudden bright
crown of quotidian fire, and then the sink
with answering crown and cusp;

the thrust of water like a rod of glass
that stuns enamel with its arrogance;
the breaking up and filling out,
the borborygmus of containers; mass,
acceleration, smell and permanence,
the ordinariness without

that turns to ordinariness within
in homely physics, domesticity.
Even of danger. When you strike
your head on a cupboard door or cut your skin
on paper you excite a kind of pity,
person and place being too alike.

You could be anywhere. Indeed you are
and always have been. It is where you go,
a mini-Mephistopheles,
a footling Faustus with familiar.
What ho, apprentice! What is there to know?
You are the master with the keys

to your own secret universe: a drawer,
a hidden box, addresses, numbers, names
and letters. All the magic charms
that gain you entrance to the inner core
of nothing/everything, the language games,
the smell of your underarms.

And far out there, responsibility
to every piece of unforgiving matter.
You run your hands across the bed
and look out from your window on the city,
draw the curtain, face the daily clutter
of the body beneath your head,

which I can't see from where I sit and gaze.
I know you are there, somewhere above
the traffic, neither near nor far
but in the middle distance which displays
a darkened rectangle that I must love
for itself and not for what we are.

THE FLIES

Forgive this garrulousness. As I write
a fat black fly crawls up the windowpane.
He feels the winter's over. Spring
anticipates itself and sets alight
worn patches of grass. The promise of warm rain
is like veins on a fly's wing.

And now a fly drops past the radiator.
The time is wrong for him. He scrambles up
fizzing furiously, leans
against the glass, revving up his motor,
then into gear and upwards. He can't stop
and think. His legs are small machines

that run until run down. I let him out.
The dot grows quickly smaller, disappears
in detail, in the dappled air.
Two distant birds swoop down and wheel about,
no bigger than flies. If I strain my ears
I hear their automatic whirr.

Look far enough, the human flies emerge . . .
I can't maintain this game of telescopes,
having never been a god
or sportsman though the hunting urge
lives in me too. I know the black fly gropes
towards his notion of the good,

his personal heap, however much it stinks;
that being here is an aesthetic choice
for those who have it, and for now
we are among this few. What the wall thinks
is my concern. We give the wall a voice.
The cut worm forgives the plough

and to the fly the plough is the cold wind
brewing beyond the Buda hills, the frost
making a belated entrance.
It's not the business of weather to be kind
nor of the market visitor to count the cost
of gypsies and of peasants.

Eternal polished faces a few streets off,
clutching embroidery or dogs for sale,
their arguments and raucous cries
exhorting us to buy the useless stuff
of lives which from here quickly lose their scale,
grow small and disappear like flies.

THE COOLEST ROOM IN THE CITY

This is the coolest room in the city,
three windows see to that, and leaves
like dark stains
lend a kind opacity
through which the whole room breathes,
and later when it rains

the windows answer anxiously,
knock for knock, and let the damp
cloud up the panes;
a cataract through which we see
reflections of a lamp
lit only when it rains.

Rooms are at their friendliest
when keeping something out. To sleep
is best. Bright chains
of water dangling at the breast
preserve their calm and keep
silence when it rains.

THE COMFORT OF ROOMS

The comfort of rooms is that they live within
and yet without the history of those
who walk across their carpets, wear new clothes
and shed their hair, bacteria and skin,
whose human walls are terrifying, thin
and useless as the petals of a rose.

An old man crawls down a short flight of stairs:
he's drying out, each time he smiles the cracks
across his face widen and come unstuck,
the paint flakes off his eyes, a muscle tears,
his marrow rattles in his bones, the layers
of vision shift in alarming parallax.

This is the parallax the windows learn
between their doubled panes. Their wings are tense,
prepared for flight, to carry the immense
hopes of the house beyond the known pattern
of its creatures. Look how the flowers burn
in the hot vase, desiring innocence.

BRIDGE PASSAGES II

A WOMAN WITH A RUG

Three loud cracks. A woman with a rug
is beating it against the rails. A rich green
flares and droops from her hands, then snap!
it's gone. It is as if she'd pulled the plug
on the street: everything is quiet again,
back within its trap.

In the nearby theatre Tuzenbach's on fire
with one of his neurotic rhapsodies.
Irina draws away from him.
He's ugly and half German. They quickly tire
of his lolloping anxiety. They tease
him because he is vague and dim

even in a passion. He seems to miss,
the tragic dimension which is rightly theirs,
their words and images,
the poems embedded in their memories.
He drifts and stumbles among chairs
down unlit passages

of dialogue. Meanwhile the woman tucks
the rug under her arm and looks across
in one of those lost moments
that can't be measured by the usual clocks,
so immobile and permanent, its loss
will never be noted in documents.

Neither will this. This moment and the next
have splintered into far too many sharp
small fragments. Unreclaimable
the bright green rug, the Baron's buried text.
Vermeer waits while time begins to warp
around his carpet-covered table

between the curtain and the string of pearls
held to the light but never quite in focus.
Irina, Masha, Olga freeze
against wild grass which has no time for girls.
The world of things remains as various
and indifferent as the leaves

in the garden which itself is lost, and where
the band is gaily signalling the fracture
of a life. A single crack is heard.
The human voice surrenders to the air:
the rug flares in the trap, its architecture
hangs clear and then is quickly blurred.

A SEA CHANGE

Far down below in next door's yard a heap
of part-dismembered cookers. On the sixth floor
shelves of plants like trailing wires
and old toupées. They've entered the big sleep,
said long goodbyes. But that's not all, there's more,
the winter merely stores desires

under the bed, in envelopes or tins.
It is a time of scuttling, wrapping close,
watching the waves of pigeons beat
against cold air. Even now something begins,
if ever so quietly, something so various
it is impossible to repeat,

that happens only once each time, perhaps
once any lifetime, a sea-change so immense
we cannot see it happen but
no one can stop thinking about it. The maps
are restless, all the boundaries are tense;
they have this feeling in the gut.

On the playground pingpong table someone scrawls
the words *New Fascists* with terrible irony.
The fearful and the ugly stalk
the spring as always. The fog's white terror calls
at dawn, remains with us. Its tyranny
lends dark edges to our talk,

but that won't stop us talking, listening.
The university bells begin to toll,
the central heating gurgles and ticks,
the starling chatters on and telephones ring
in nearby rooms. The world is audible
at last above its politics

and talks to itself. Behind the frosted glass
someone takes a shower. These things are done
precisely as before but feel
a little different now. The yellow grass
is its own particular shade. The railings run
more purposefully and reveal

precise configurations in the gaps.
It matters that you give things the right name
and measure their extent, their power.
It happens rarely. Now's the time perhaps
for understanding what remains the same.
The water thunders in the shower.

IN A STRONG LIGHT

Behind the shower-curtain thunder sharpens
into light. The douche destroys
the human figure and does its best
to murder space. Everything that happens
is the echo of something else, which merely deploys
your shoulder and your breast.

The white striations shimmer without contour
exhaled in the relieved sigh
of water. You dissolve in pools.
The sun breaks on bare twigs in a winter
truce between opposing powers of grey.
Even as the body cools

the room still breathes its freshness and the scent
of soap continues to haunt the walls. Alone
the body loses resolution,
and feels at home in its abandonment.
The lost flesh settles down against the bone
with the lightness of a cushion.

To feel complete and disparate at once
is rarely possible. Think how the sun
breaks down a house yet makes it glow
in burning fragments or deconstructs a fence
into mere rhythm. All the harmony is gone,
but something leaps where shadows throw

their careless and flat members. Your body is warm
and slopes so gently. Hands have narrowed it
to wrists and ankles, formed the bolder
curvatures of your temple and your arm,
explored your ears, lovingly parodied
your brittle collarbone and shoulder.

To snap out of the body, find it stiff
or burned or crippled, to become objective
as sun or water are, will not
completely cancel out a world. And if
it did there'd still remain the live
arguments of the planet:

the child in the pushchair; quiet empty places
where the streets are full of dogshit; hats and shoes;
grotesques met in an underpass;
the delicate careful pity of faces
in memory or mirror; the everyday news
of bridges, trees and grass.

SMOG

An idea so macabre it cannot picture
its own desperation. Who pre-recorded
all her birthday greetings years ahead,
chorus after chorus? Who threatened us
with euthanasia and longed to die
and did so, out of synch and out of luck?
I have the tape still. Would not a single chorus
have been enough, leaving behind perhaps
some plain instruction to rewind each year,
to do this in remembrance . . . Well, people have crazy notions,
they want the living to miss them naturally,
but everything grows back or is resurfaced,
all smoothed out by the traffic. It is winter:
a smog compounded of Trabants and the Danube,
these words drift through blank fields of noise
grey and elegiac among buildings,
cling to dirty windows or to collars
turned against air. 'I love smog', someone scrawls
across a huddled car. The letters start to run,
gather force past ridged deposits,
breathe and leave a coating on the lungs.

THE LOST MONEY

I'm lying down flat on the floor just reading
when the money starts to fall out of my pocket,
not merely money—keys and tickets, shreds
of paper handkerchiefs—but it's the money
that appears most real, and I keep thinking
my pockets are not deep enough because it trickles
through my fingers even through the cloth,
and I remember or redream the time
a pickpocket once in the Tuileries
slipped her hand into my pocket and I
grabbed at it, her scrawny wrist
a fish fresh out of water, the coins like scales
spilling from my pocket till I wake.

If it comes to that I guess I've never known
the value of cash, unlike my parents
one of whom was paid in lard, the other
perhaps in salt, I can't remember which,
and they were anxious that I might go hungry,
which was annoying then, particularly
since I felt guilty, having made them worry
about having to go and get more money,
and here I am at forty, vaguely aware
of something slipping from my pocket, a dream
or dreams which feel too much like cash,
but go on reading, gathering up loose change
and thinking it's all right and still not worrying.

Unlike I suppose the pair that I keep seeing
drifting about town. Let me describe them to you.
The man has a beard and lurches violently
from one place to another. His beard is short,
his face square. While she stands at the bus stop
in apparent indifference, he gets down on his knees
and peers between her legs, from front, from rear.
She stands unmoving, looks away. He lurches
again, growls at a passing woman, mutters,
then resumes his work. The bus arrives. He sways
on to the platform. She turns round, her cut lip
and bulging eye immobile, follows him.
Next time she stands before the subway entrance
and he appears behind a pillar, beckons,
and she starts to walk in his direction.
Her trousers are striped, her jumper a dull yellow.
In the nearby block a woman takes a dirt tray
down to the shute marked Rubbish
and discovers a human couple in the primal
position. Darkness. A hasty pardon.
She withdraws. When he does, it is to piss
into the shute and when the pair pack up
they pass into the street, continue their game
of follow-my-leader. Her cheeks are heavy, swollen,
shining, faintly blue, her bruised lips bear
a faint glaze of saliva which disturbs me
as if loose change were spilling from her mouth.

SEVEN POEMS FROM THE HUNGARIAN OF OTTÓ ORBÁN

(b.1936)

HOUSE AND HOME

A house, a home, Horatius, Illyés, indeed, *the lot* . . .
But chiefly the subterranean pool, freckled with silk and velvet:
an adolescent's image of earth's lap
or what lies beneath that triangle of grass—
the brimstone path to hell, that opalescent lake
with German tourists and chippies along its shore,
in which I dip myself each year to gauge
how much my life has managed to squeeze from me.
Summer: the rustic club is now a stalwart piston, the male member
proudly pumps the yielding medium, no problem;
he is happy to be his own way, truth and life—
great mushroom clouds cannot daunt the random explorer
whose mighty lightning zaps into the lap of the material;
followed by darkness and nothing, and nothing and darkness . . .

BENEATH THE THUNDERING ROOF

Hamline University, St Paul, Minnesota

No fantasy more inscrutable than that which exists;
what we claim to know is merely a membrane, oceans of cells either side—
too bad we should live our lives in terror of it
and so we pretend it is human, and give it a sense of humour . . .
Who knows what life should compensate us for, why now?
why war, why the hospitals, the diploma we failed to obtain?
Too late, too late, sniggers Professor Orbán of Hungary,
he has already felt the dark current of air, and even though crippled,
he is, compared to his mad teenage self, practically free . . .
Should he sell this for bits of luminous trash sold on television?
Here I sit in the golden age of the empire, the air-conditioning humming,
teaching the fraught psychology of vandals to simple-faced Romans—
more serious though is the roof, cracked and thundering with imperial aircraft,
which even the limestone column of my spine cannot shore up.

THE SNOWS OF YESTERYEAR

Where is Mr Orbán, last year's visiting professor?
Where is his queer accent, his strange opinions?
Deep, deep, deep in the hill he sleeps,
like other citizens of the Spoon River.
I contemplate this man in boots and anorak,
whose grey curls peek out under his fur hat;
an ageing party waiting for the bus to take him to St Paul—
I would not notice him were he not me . . .
Incredible that my past should belong to him,
still more incredible, that his is mine . . .
Some third person is writing my poems, one who knows my
  obsessions intimately,
before his eyes the orange malleable lava of the day before yesterday
is hardening to a dark basalt grey that one might study,
and the dumb snow falls like lint on the open wound of the world.

A VISIT TO ROOM 104

I saw how death pursued its calling in peacetime;
carving fine detail, a vigilant minor craftsman:
one lump on the thighbone, one on the brain, one by the eyes—
he worked in fine temper and whistled a tune down the oxygen
    tube . . .
All our lives we prepare for the great Titus Dugovic scene
where we perform a spectacular double-twist dive off the castle
    ramparts
and make an impression on our descendants—
a downbeat ending comes as a surprise . . .
We're not prepared for the fact that our bodies pack up—
that we find no space in bed for our hands or our legs,
that we spend the whole night on a bed of sharp nails, tossing and
    turning . . .
mud then or spirit? The choice of the romantic,
of the archer with one eye shut, of the eschatologist—
from death's point of view all things are mud, even the spirit.

THE FATHER OF THE PEOPLE

Which deified monarch had fewer restraints or more power?
His was the way, the truth and the life, but chiefly the death;
his world was as simple as Russian Roulette,
the red ball, obedience: the black, execution . . .
A brief generation, to see his fallen statues' living original—
the short-assed, vengeful, industrious genius of organization,
who dickered with his penknife in a functioning watch,
because he failed to grasp the ideal in whose name he murdered.
Divinity requires a godlike imagination,
a pinch of poetry to go with the hard-line of strategy—
conscience and soul are not merely words in a spectrum,
sooner or later the lie starts to rot in the firm-looking binding,
and chronically sneezing, time, the monumental mason, carves on
  the tombstone
of common memory: Xerxes; Capone; the once fearful name of the
  emperor.

WITCHFINDER GENERAL

In the imagined TV-series produced by neo-conservative ideology
Jean-Jacques Rousseau (quiet atmospheric music) goes for a walk
in the wood and finds a casket, opens it, and out flies the devil
who wears a new disguise each century, now Robespierre, now
Hitler,
and beats this vale of tears to a bloody pulp of millions of victims,
and with a blade honed on mass ideology trims beard and neck at
once.
To be sure, by the time he gets home late at night, history is
exhausted
and bored of the bloodbath at Vendée and Katyn Forest;
it longs for a bit of home-cooking and TV in front of the fire . . .
The new fundamentalist of the age is a disappointed egghead,
a curved sabre forged on the anvil of elite universities in his hand,
while a sparkling inscription on the fine cutting edge of his wit
reminds him
of the address and the postcode of hell: Paris, 1789.

A ROMAN CONSIDERS THE CHRISTIANS

May the gods forgive me but I really can't abide them.
Their idea is a great one, but look at them all:
a bunch of quarrelsome highbrows picking their noses,
who, under the spell of their thesis, would if they could
be hard-line dictators, all for the sake of tolerance naturally,
who'd not kill with weapons but with murderous disdain,
while breeding their own sloppy aristocracy,
along with other oppressive, life-hating state institutions . . .
So, let me embellish this with a gesture—a fig for them all!
Just one little problem: the starved lion bawling in the arena . . .
There are plenty with vision, but they are the ones prepared to be
  eaten
in dust-clouds of water-cannon, where out of the screaming and
  bloodshed
something emerges . . . the same thing? the worse? or the better?
the gods only know, if they know, what lies in the future . . .

BRIDGE PASSAGES III

NACHTMUSIK

Miraculous night when all the lights go out
except the bulbs on the high galleries,
and the radio spills its beans
of rattling music and surrounds the heart,
when the blood within the veins begins to freeze
into serene patterns.

The beautiful sad melancholy voices
of a conjectural landscape, Heimat. The lull
of belonging. To act,
to make things happen, to make choices
are all conditions of the beautiful
and the exact.

The air itself dissolves. The wind is pushing
it around so it changes consistency,
allows more rain, more light,
more darkness through. Nature keeps gatecrashing
the city parties, devalues the currency
of our affairs which legislate

for the predictable, the violence
of skin and fist, and the executives
of reason. Even nausea
begins in nature, and the elements
line up numerically like captives
in an alien sphere.

But music, what to do with you
now lights are out? You always simplify,
invoke. The crudest song
still rings a bell which echoes through
the system and proclaims that though we die
we nevertheless belong.

It doesn't tell us where, that is the catch,
the air always dissolves. The wind allows
the notes to congregate
then blows the gaff on them and leaves a snatch
of something without form. The empty noise
of radio waves. It's getting late.

I'm putting the words in order, miles away
from any sea. I read the papers through
and hear the creak of doors.
The foreign airs are moving: *lullay, lullay.*
The tune billows and scrapes. Such singers do
without accompaniment or scores.

BRIDGE PASSAGE

You could be anywhere. The broken islands,
the excellence of fog from off the sea,
Well, I was there once, by the pier
where a loud amusement arcade lit the sands
and on the beach lay an abandoned body
and discarded tins of beer.

And the sea just went on mumbling as it does,
lightly clicking its tongue against black stone,
and everything was out there: lust
and loneliness, the neon razzmatazz
of passing time, and time too passing on
to things a passage can adjust.

But certainties remained beyond its range.
The rubbing away, the spartan cheerfulness,
the small talk of cold waves,
preserve an ambience from too much change
too suddenly unless, beyond the ness,
it rears the emptiness of graves.

The waves are ridges, roofs at their own pitch,
waiting in long queues. You move inland
with the incoming tide, arrive
at shallow docks and promenades, at rich
hotels and boarding houses, and the grand
perspectives of the downward drive.

Inland again. The trunk roads. Towns beyond
the motorway. The service station. Lights
and more lights. Lamplit necklaces
of roads in conurbations, brilliant blond
commercial signs. Estates and building sites
and po-faced sixties terraces.

Recounting these things tells you just what is,
a gazetteer with no particulars
in view but Europe's lingua franca
of luminous directions, boundaries,
and the fixed stare of endless waves of cars
cresting in truck and petrol tanker.

But this too tells you nothing, though behind
the roof-racks something glimmers. A thin line
where islands hang and stare at rings
of water vaguely pressing at some blind
corner where things must quickly find a sign
to live by, to remain mere things.

THE SERVICE OF REMEMBRANCE

I still remember you. The oldest words.
You're sitting in the kitchen like a wraith
who passes easily through the wall.
You're weather now, part of the afterwards,
the having been. Yours is the narrow faith
that leaves me empty, insubstantial,

queasily watching the sea remove
a mouthful of small pebbles and then throw
back the remainder. A figure stands
by an open window. Outside the branches wave
to no one in particular. Their leaves blow
one way then another, hands

to match the one grasping the windowsill.
The slight breeze lifts a few hairs from your temple
in a kind of farewell gesture.
Some cars are crawling up the hill.
People are coming home. There is a simple
characteristic posture

against the moving world. What is memory
but scent wedded to immobility?
A man enters the house, a sparrow
flies on to his shoulders. This territory
is dangerously laced. It's not just pity,
but Eros, the boy with the arrow

who threatens the stillness here in Colindale,
in north-west London, anno imprecise.
He shoots the bird. The time we pass
has made us valuable, fit for sale
to one another at the knockdown price
of desire as common as grass.

So now I see the kitchen clear but can't
remember where the usual things are kept,
I can't find anything at all
though I know too well that something quite important
is hidden in the room, a life so stripped
it's almost frozen beyond recall.

And this is where we are, at least for now,
except today a quiet breathing heats
the window, whose wing opens
to movements of the air, and a light bough
is tossing in the wind and a few sheets
on the line lift their white hems.

APPROPRIATIONS

ENGLISH WORDS

My first three English words were AND, BUT, SO:
they were exotic in my wooden ear,
like Froebel blocks. Imagination made
houses of them, just big enough to hang
a life on. Genii from a gazetteer
of deformations or a *sprechgesang*:
somehow it was possible to know
the otherness of people and not be afraid.

Once here, the words arranged their quaint occasions,
Minding their Manners, Waiting in the Queues
at Stops and Hatches, I got to know their walls,
their wallpaper and decorative styles,
their long louche socks, their sensible scuffed shoes.
Peculiar though: their enigmatic smiles
and sideways looks troubled my conversation
swimming in clouds above the steam of kettles.

You say a word until it loses meaning
and taste the foreignness of languages,
your own included. Sheer inanity
of idiom: the lovely words are dead,
their magic gone, evaporated pages.
But this too is a kind of spell: unread,
the vocables coagulate and sting,
glow with their own electricity.

I cannot trust words now. One cultivates
the sensuous objects in a locked museum:
their sounds are dangerous and must be heard
voluptuously, but behind thick glass.
Their emptiness appals one. One is dumb
with surprise at their inertia, their crass
hostility. They are beautiful opiates,
as brilliant as poppies, as absurd.

SALT

It begins in salt, a pinch of white
added to a mound on a tablecloth
in a friendless boarding-house, where she talks
of striptease and he looks vaguely embarrassed,
makes sucking noises with his mouth,
and hates the elaborately curtained and terraced
six-room establishment with its sixty-watt light
and its proximity to coastal walks.

It begins here, eating out the centre
of the past, an indifferent turning-away,
leaving an ache for the vanished
that goes on vanishing, eroding under
wind and sea, an ancient fishlike bay,
a resort that ages badly and turns blander
with each year that heads for winter,
and still the story isn't finished.

Sealed tobacco tins and open drawers
of pale devices, magazines that burn
in hands, the smell of adult beds.
A lit room in a window, the reflection
of a boy writhing like a worm,
the black panes each with its clear section
of interior, of walls and doors
that bear the familiar burdens of his head.

This was the parental home the sea
brought in, its end in its beginning
tail-in-mouth eternally. This cold
and even light that levels out the tones
of summer autumn winter and the spring
within a narrow harmony of bones
and fossils will lend domesticity
to secret lives. And now they can be told.

BODIES

A brawny driver with enormous hands
is injured in an accident. At night
he shows his scar. His wife looks frail
as she describes the junction and the dark
where it all happened. Her eyes are bright,
dilate with impact, her shadow stark.
She begins to dance beside him where he stands—
immense, protective, vastly out of scale.

It is hard to know just where to place a thing.
A paper tissue blown against
a branch, the sea's seminal calm
shoving and caving. On the long settee
a couple smooches; a blonde-rinsed
girl, the man moustached and military
like a conjuror. They cling
together swaying palm to palm.

Every night a new performance.
Every night a new forging of links.
There's something in it quite methodical
and rather less than modest.
He wonders what the heavy driver thinks,
and what that frailness looks like when undressed,
what insinuations make palms dance
and how such largeness must be magical.

Like broken glass, the sea-spray
splinters, leaves her bodywork, her slap
of brakes. All couples are accidents,
mothers and fathers, bathers on the beach
among the towels in which they wrap
their changing bodies. They will teach
their children modesty. Their flesh is clay
and kneadable. It smells of innocence.

MR REASON

Dear Mr Reason, hook-nosed and Punch-jawed,
is nevertheless handsome and a hero
to the class of ten-year-olds who love to hear
his voice expand like an enormous football.
He is the ultimate inflated zero
of their short experience. Sometimes he'll call
on God in accents mild or cry him abroad
with trumpetry. He is their Chanticleer

and Unicorn. But now, hair powdered
by the blue dusk falling through the glass, he seems
an angel of some sort. The milk they hold
in their soft hands is what is drunk in heaven.
He speaks their names and summons them through dreams
of being good—Nigel, Sarvin, Trevor,
Jimmy, Wendy—tripping light-padded
among their words, gathering in his fold.

St Catherine's Lighthouse, Alum Bay, the Castle
where the king once slept. This miniature
isle of brightness is the heart of something
so indigenous it drags at small hearts
with reminiscences of furniture
in old men's rooms. There he too waits, a part
of sunlight, dusk, the seashore and the puzzle
of archaic words and comfortable singing.

His terror too: once in the pavilion
the groundsman found a mess, a human mess,
quite foul and brown, no bigger than an egg.
His furious inquest made them all ashamed.
But now well-being, warmth and doziness
creep over children pleased with being named
in Mr Reason's grace. Next afternoon
they'll hear a sermon by the Reverend Legge.

MISS PICKERING

Miss Pickering, like a pickled walnut,
dithered among palettes, swam in a haze
of thin spittle, shrank behind glass
till she attained a precious quality.
She coaxed and tutted tiny words of praise,
A very nice thing, dear and *Oh how pretty!*
and her pearly eyes opened and shut
on the big room and swallowed up the class.

They would, if they could, have learned from her
some grace or delicacy, but colours ran
in grey pools over scored lines
that represented nothing and were graceless.
Their hands remained stubbornly simian.
They dreamed of running fingers over a dress
or exploring the intricacies of long hair
through endless and romantic lunchtimes.

The girls themselves were consciously superior.
Their bodies moved beyond Miss Pickering
answering questions she would never ask.
They'd take from her as much of delicacy
as they required, then pass on, leave her twittering
about the small bones of a leaf, or the lacy
complications of flowers. They saw much clearer
the powers around them and took larger risks.

I think of Miss Pickering dead, a needle in
the darkest of haystacks, of filigree,
of egg and dart, of finial and crocket
and the worrying precisions of needlepoint
like white foam stitched to the borders of the sea
riding its back astride the slopping paint.
It's something, after all, to sidle in
and keep a little in so small a pocket.

SEASIDE POSTCARD

The sea contracted to a water pistol
is pointed at a child's head and explodes
in laughter. It is autumn. Leaves litter
the pavements. Dry, they are as delicate
as dead skin. Even the wet roads
ignite under our feet and store the late
weak sun till evening comes. A dark pastel
obliterates them all. The nights are bitter

as fine chocolate and as sweet. The games
continue in and out of private gardens,
round fat public trees. Manners grow stiff
at neighbours' open gates. The scout huts beckon
their lost hearties: small boys, churchmen, wardens.
Front rooms fill with TV. The american
comics dance across the screen, trail names
of power through grey and white in low relief.

The child appears, wide-eyed as an icon,
learning the words, staring at a space
beyond the inner one of Now. He wears a comic
pullover, hair parted in horns of light.
The wind is striking at his open face,
gets in among the teeth. The sea is white
against the rows of houses, waves break on
walls and grey-green tide marks stain the brick.

The situation has been well prepared,
preserved in frozen worlds of Beezers, Toppers,
Beanos and Dandys. A dog leaps from a gate
with sharp teeth snapping, worrying at his heels.
The words have gathered in his heart like coppers
which can be spent now, freely. He appeals
for help, his hands extended, running scared.
His yell is comic and articulate.

A PICTURE OF MY PARENTS WITH THEIR FIRST TELEVISION

I see them before the television, the proud owners
of a wooden case in which the four-o-five
presents its milky versions of success
with the last official faces of a time
that was always more dead than alive,
when Hanratty cleaned the windows and a crime
was solved by men with briefcases and bowlers,
when gentlemen made jokes in evening dress.

They fought their way to this, to Lady Barnett
to Bernard Braden and John Freeman, Kathie Kay
and Alan Breeze, to all those names of power
that solved nothing but could somehow fill
the hours before they slipped away
to private lives which grew more private still,
past old reliable faces by which they set
their clocks precisely to the latest hour.

Some blurred depth in their eyes won't come to rest:
perhaps they're trapped in what they bought,
in all their trappings, in the slim white frame
of the square photograph they sent back home
to show the television. Now they're caught
and solemn. Slowly they become
the stillness by which they are both possessed.
They're listening intently for a name

which once had power, on lips that formed the sound
in darkened flats, in beds in which they slept
and touched each other. Some act of violence
has pitched them here before the screen.
The actors know their speeches, are adept
at pulling faces, know when to go. They've been
elsewhere and are there still, on neutral ground,
of which this patch of grey is evidence.

LOSING

We lose each other everywhere:
the children in department stores
return as parents, *fils et père*
collide by the revolving doors.

The pavements' litter, burning flakes
of bonfires, tickets and franked stamps,
the fragile image drops and breaks,
the fugitive awakes, decamps.

The carriages uncouple, trucks
return unladen, suits appear
on vacant charitable racks,
the shelves of darkened stockrooms clear,

skin lifts and peels. A cake of soap.
The human lamps, the nails, the hair,
the scrapbooks' chronicles of hope
that lose each other everywhere.

BRIDGE PASSAGES IV

A GAME OF STATUES

The pond seems to be still, but everywhere
small points of tension gather and stretch.
Dead leaves float in cowls.
The slab breaks up. The foil begins to tear.
The grass is smeared with snowdrops, bluebells, vetch.
The air is a parliament of fowls.

Broad avenues and city parks are dressed
to kill. Houses put on airs and graces.
A hidden population of statues
emerges from the shadows to be pressed
between the brickwork till the terraces
are packed with ancient vices and virtues

pouting and posturing. Their breasts and biceps curve
against the sunlight which first called them out,
even the crippled ones assume
survival rights. Forsaking their reserve,
they brandish their stigmata. Blank faces shout
from pediments, burst into bloom.

An air of celebration. Time replies
with memory. She mounts a ruined staircase
through heaps of rubble. She has come
back from the camps and wagons to surprise
the world. Each broken window wears her face,
her footsteps are a muffled drum.

She knows what she has to do. No need for food,
affection is the cure: the street's hot breath
on neck and earlobe, words and sighs.
They let her go. The air in the room is good
but better still to pass through it, through death,
to this demi-paradise

of iron, stone and stucco. Across the city
thousands are marching past, and poking heads
and arms through niches, waiting there
for common symbols of eternity.
Think of them struggling in their vertical beds
against the continual nightmare

of the wall. The whole street seems to pose
and catch the light. Across the ruffled pond
birds are frozen into screams
of joy. A single, vaguely comatose
statue holds real flowers in her hand.
The flowers are dying as she dreams.

STREET ENTERTAINMENT

The March wind turns up suddenly and shreds
loose canvas on the awnings. Inverted flames
of cloth billow and long to escape
the world of definitions. Even people's heads
seem to be on fire, grow lion's manes,
echoing some comical shape

of terror. These are territorial wars.
You half expect them to rise and spit at each other
just as the rain is doing now,
to arch their backs and growl. Well, here are cars
hunched and growling, part of the same weather,
low clouds learning to bellow

with best or worst. You should have expected this.
You should have worn your coat or slipped the brolly
into your pocket. They are so neat,
so easy to carry. The weather has given notice
it intends to change. It thinks of human folly
as a faint tickling under its feet.

The street entertainers are out. One old beggar
blows his harmonica so faintly the sound
is blown back in his face. A boy
with a recorder stands before a figure
of Mercury, with his schoolcap on the ground
like an abandoned toy.

The ones that interest me are a pair
dressed vaguely as musketeers, in puritan hats
and rose pink gowns. They wield
long sticks. They do nothing but stare
at the growing crowd, till someone puts
a coin into the box, when a wild

mechanical movement seizes them and they
are frozen once again in attitudes
of sinister aggression.
Their faces mimic something, yet are empty.
A girl runs between them and poses. The crowd
laughs at her silly expression.

I'm merely a reporter whose truth lies
in diction clear as water. In the pool
which I imagine by my shoes
I try to see my features, read my eyes.
It ripples. My face is indistinguishable,
the water darkens like a bruise.

NATIONAL ANTHEM

The spring begins an age of festivals:
the outbreaks and foundations, liberations,
appointed days, appointed modes
of putting on. The flags hang from the walls.
The weather bustles by. The operations
of the state. The empty roads.

The corridors too are empty though the sun
has laid its fingers underneath each door
to beckon us out. It's quiet:
something bothers the sky. Something remains undone.
April now but it could be May: Nature
that great abstraction is set

before us: small green arguments of leaves,
the proclamations of blossom on each branch,
the flowers with their furious dance.
Meaning! Meaning! they jostle, Whoever believes
in us, must give us meaning! An avalanche
of meaning! Let us have significance!

They shimmer and shake in silence before windows,
in tall black rectangles beyond which only
gods and geometricians see.
I too am sitting in one. Windows close
and open, doors swing to. There is nobility
in loneliness and vacancy,

but meaning too is rooted in a place,
is like a statue always looking past
the same old clump of trees
winter and summer, the same look on its face.
How long can faces at the windows last?
They disappear by slow degrees

each disappearance quick in its own terms.
Mother, father, child. They call out names
that no one understands but them.
They wear their universal forms,
their worn-out clothes. The sunlight frames
each figure like a theorem.

We're here, such as we are. We will be missed.
Some children gather opposite, look down
into the courtyard where
music's playing. A lone saxophonist
proffers the national anthem. The notes are blown
random, slow, into the air.

THE CHAIRS

Where did you stay that winter?
(Singapore? Hyderabad?)
No, we waited in the snow,
All dressed up, nowhere to go.

Where did you sit while waiting?
(In a taxi? In a train?)
We took the armchair from the hall
But did not feel we'd moved at all.

What did you think of, waiting?
(Summer sun and fresh sea air?)
All we thought of was the end
Of summer and the north-east wind.

But didn't you sing while waiting?
(Christmas comes but once a year.)
We ourselves, we couldn't sing
But we heard others carolling.

Then sing now. What have you to sing?
We'll sing of leaving. When we've gone
You can do as we have done.
Here's a chair for sitting on.

THE WEATHER AT THE DOOR

I

Wind at the door—a furious man knocking
enters your head and takes a turn
about the room. He leaves you shaken.
Your eyes are red, your cheeks burn,
your skeleton has shrunk to hard dry skin.
The wind goes out and half your life is taken
in a gesture. It is both refreshing and shocking.
You'll wait for him again and let him in.

2

The snow with its ground glass which penetrates
to secret places wounds you with its cold,
disturbs your diction, has you reaching for
the comfort of worn words. You're growing old.
You're comforted by known loves, ratty garments.
The snow is falling from another shore,
another life invades your own. The night
is closing in on beds in small apartments.

3

What brilliant sunlight! You have to close your eyes
against the windows with their fields
of cloth and gold. The world turns delicate
as fingers under tables, a hand yields
to the pressure of a neck. The nakedness
of grass. Leaves of slate
across the scalp. The soft earth in disguise.
The breast in blossom blown beneath the dress.

4

The fog breaks up infinitesimal
in particles of moisture, not quite snow
nor rain either but har, a mad Scottische
on moor or loch's edge, and you hardly know
the place. Like hoardings, all the images
dissolve into some system, find a niche
in the imagination, the decimal
points of love on virginal grey pages.

5

Then rain, the hoariest metaphor which shows
the balance of fertility and pain
and turns both to desire. The streets
are swimming in it. It fills the drain,
runs out, tumbles in brief pleats
like shaken curtains. The wind blows
against the glass, begging to be let in.

BRIDGE PASSAGES V

RAIN

Rain all night. Those sitting in the roof
can hear it talking but they cannot tell
the nature of its message.
It broods and blows, gathers, grows smooth
and seamless. In the stairwell
and the basement passage

it spreads as damp, the closing smell of sweat.
A fly is buzzing round and round. You wouldn't think
a creature small as that
could emit so thick a blare. It deals in threat
and sings of filth. You seem to hear the stink
of old outhouses and dried shit.

Those who speak are moving in the houses,
closing doors, wiping their faces. One picks up
a paper, another puts one down.
Familiar looks, good nights. A car cruises
by outside. Lost and out of step,
history leaves the empty town.

The rain is a mad typist clattering out
endless streams of letters without a break,
littered with quaint symbols.
You can't pronounce the words, nor can you shout
for lack of vowels. The language starts to ache
and slowly crumbles.

If rain talks it talks nonsense. We lie beside
each other on the bed and think of all
who lie there listening.
Bodies and bodies and the rain outside.
The small intimate whispers of the wall.
The loud fly's translucent wing.

CHINESE WHITE

Do you remember that scene in Ashes and Diamonds *where*
the hero rushes forward through the clotheslines and bleeds
to death among the sheets? Or was it
in Canal *(I can't remember now.) A square*
of white turns slowly red. The redness fades
to black and white. The picture is a composite,

a form of poster. The War, the Resistance,
something about betrayal, all mixed up
in a child's mind who didn't see
the war, for whom it is a haunting presence
of sheets and blood. An image hangs and drops
in a grey passageway or alley.

His name was Zbigniew, and he wore dark glasses,
and later he jumped from a train (a true life fact)
because, well, Poles are like that,
they get drunk, morose, et cetera. The girl who kisses
the boy was blonde as always. Was it an act
of bravery him getting shot

or cowardice? We could look it up in books
but that is not the point (we pull our serious face)
but something in the falling, the how
and where of it. And so wherever one looks
the same old images return and find their place,
a square, an alleyway, a row

of ordinary houses suddenly still and hot
and people falling lying as if on a square
of film. You see the victim's head
as someone aims and shoots him, and you cut
to tanks or bodies or a sheet hung out to air,
a white square slowly turning red.

FUNERAL ORATION

The objects are on stage: their shadows link.
The sunlight turns the towel opposite
into the likeness of a man,
but the gallery is empty, on the brink
of someone's entrance. Empty chairs sit,
waiting. Someone draws a curtain.

Perhaps they'll step out and sit down. Perhaps
a child, more likely the blind woman who
has always lived here. The ledge
is hung with assorted greenery that drips
between the iron. Leaves bubble through
the railings. Somewhere there's a bridge

between the actor and his ghosts. A voice.
Some trick of speech. A broken window speaks
like tinkling glass, a bullet spits
into a cherub's puffed and vacant face.
Even the old rusted awnings creak
in chorus. Everything falls to bits,

the plaster and the stairs, the life within
the rooms, but one still steps out for a breath
of fresh air on the gallery.
It is as if he stepped out of his skin
or casually walked out of his death,
past the neat artillery

of railings, past the chairs, until he found
the one reserved for him, that had been waiting
like an open vowel
to close beneath him. And when the light turns round
you begin to see the human form, the sitting
figure hidden in the towel.

A WALK ACROSS FIELDS

for Winifred Upchurch

Not to have known the landscape was my loss—
a scoop of cloud held all the land, the sky
was panes of glass, and rain in quiet gutters
shook like leaves.

The streets for walking, rooms for dreams, the grass
in parks for small adventures: one could die
in forests, magic castles, doorways, broken shutters,
in urban graves

where books held all the secrets. Wind blows across
the river. The trees are bending. Thick clouds lie
like wadding on them. Distant predators
move in droves

beyond the bands of rain. The sleeping palace
waked to potent thunder. The children dry
their clothes. I think of parents, grandmothers,
the natural loves.

BRIDGE PASSAGES VI

BURNING STUBBLE AT SZIGLIGET

We stepped out on the balcony. The sky
had grown romantic and the breaking pods
and stalks were rapid volleys of light.
The air was damp, but somewhere it was dry
as fury, spitting heat. The little roads
were silent and the trees clung tight

to the black park, which had for years been theirs.
The statues held their poses even though
no one was there to see them, lost
in dark and dark grey, minding their own affairs.
The alien world lay immediately below,
and waited patient at its post.

Deep alizarin crimson, bleeding down
to ochre, orange, yellow. Spectacular
colours and a crackling rain
which wasn't rain but something overthrown.
The light was falling like the morning star:
the sons of light were dark again.

On lamp-posts, upside down, hung shrunken skins
which once were men. Tractors like tanks appeared
and crushed the street to crisp white flour.
A woman was kicking a corpse. The thin grey curtains
of smoke trembled and behind them cleared
a space for buildings and a shower

of broken stucco. A sentence broke apart,
each word a promise made in any street
and broken here. I couldn't sleep.
Beyond the park I heard the firing start
and the snap snap snap was tiny running feet
of shrews and mice, of lives held cheap.

Well, it was tidy and the cheapness ours,
our cheap hands on the pillars, our cheap eyes
seeking the heart of flames between
the foreground darkness. Now for a few hours
the fields would burn and the tall smoke would rise
as delicate as mesh to screen

the lake beyond the fields, the towns astride
the motorway, high white estates like teeth,
the factories, our balcony,
and all the others who had come outside
to stand by blazing windows ranged beneath
the rolling smoke, the thin grey sea.

WILD GARDEN

Vadkert. The wild garden. Sunlight. Notations
on a stave, an airless music in the ears
of bridges, masonry and trees
which spread themselves like railway stations,
heading off towards the park to hear
plain footsteps, plain itineraries.

But who are these, these wild ones in the garden,
the calves and chickens, peacocks, ducks and rams
at whom pre-conscious children wave
fistfuls of crumbs, for whom the old unburden
themselves of stale loaves? Why do the rattling trams
carry them both towards this grave

ceremonial greenness? Such incongruity
is simply another game of let's pretend
that nothing happens. It calls you back,
reminds you how you too felt gravity
tugging at your spine like an old friend
who gave you a playful smack

then set you up again. A mother waits
by an empty push chair. Her child puts a finger through
the chicken wire. Birds peck at it
disappointed. The menagerie congregates
around us, black, white, purple, peacock blue:
brilliant and profligate.

Happiness is very simple really,
it flows out of the horn of plenty, abundant
as rain or grass but wilder, rarer
than the rainbow. Are you here with me?
Will you stand beside me for ever, as constant
as these farmyard birds and fairer

than the peacock, startled and beautiful,
with his improbable Japanese elegance?
In the city they're counting votes
and learning how to speak. Feel gravity pull
your sleeve to closer acquaintance with all gardens.
From this distance you may make notes

on the society of worms and ants and clods
in their private infinity of lives
lived in terror of the creatures
of the garden. And beyond them lie the woods,
the lakes, the sea and the enormous waves
on which we inscribe our human features.

IN MEMORIAM SÁNDOR WEÖRES

I met him only once. So light and grey,
his handshake hardly registered. He might
have been a speck of household dust,
his absence the most palpable quality.
He settled in the chair and made a slight
noise, as if he'd caught a crust

of dry bread in his throat. He signed my book
in a childish trembling hand. He was depressed.
His cat had died. He could hardly speak
but smiled, shyly, vaguely. He had the look
of a February morning, waiting, dressed,
for some final naked event to break,

when he, at last, could be that sublimate
his body had aspired to, simply vapour
burning above a mound of ash.
But this would be a pyre to celebrate
his substance—words and pen and ink and paper
all the luminous trash

of magic and art. The conjuror could take
a parasol and out of it create
an ecosystem, or beneath
the parasol, meander in the wake
of *realpolitik* and contemplate
its dreadful colonnade of teeth.

His invented psyche was both male and female.
Two breasts had risen somewhere in his breast
like towers, so that when he took breath
two bodies rose and fell with it. His pale
shadow left the boy, the light caressed
his skin. He couldn't tell life from death.

He never was good company, would disappear
without one noticing and be discovered
wrapped in a blanket on the tramline
in the middle of the night. He never was there
and nowhere else. Everything he suffered
glowed in the language, turned to wine,

but such a wine as city children, bred
in stinking courtyards, would find in the street,
and when they drunk it, they would know
their nonsense validated by the dead.
He was the poet they'd queue up to meet,
in whose lost shadow they could grow.

TWO RONDEAUS:

1 Unter den Linden

In Unter den Linden and Wenceslas Square
the candles wink their *laissez-faire*,
people are trampling over borders,
packing their luggage. Cassette recorders
hiss like steam in the cold air,

cameras roll and spokesmen prepare
brief noncommittal statements, tear
pages from notebooks and wait for orders.
Prisons open: prisoners and warders
   mix in Unter den Linden.

In Prague and Budapest they wear
rosettes, wave flags. A furious year
gathers to a close. The wind disorders
ships of state and fleets of boarders.
Men link hands, dance and boldly stare
   across Unter den Linden.

2 Clumsy Music

A clumsy music: years lurch on
and fugitive clocks on the run
must settle debts by Hogmanay.
At Christmas guilty parents pay
the devil who pays debts to none.

Important things remain undone,
the boxes open: one by one
their ghosts are spirited away:
the piper stands by set to play
  his clumsy music,

artificial yet homespun,
a rondeau much like this, begun
in hope as much as fear, to lay
his fears and keep wild hopes at bay
with dancing, linking hands, best done
  to clumsy music.

DIARY

from the Hungarian of Ágnes Nemes Nagy

Mind

I know I have no reasonable grounds
for thinking, but watch the thoughts as they go round.
And since contempt's appropriate to the act
mindlessly I trust to intellect.

Nightmare

From a world of rotting rags and clout
the marsh-light of cold reason flashes out,
plays on the corpse, the softening skull beneath,
and illuminates its naked row of teeth.

Revenge

He who cannot take revenge,
nor yet forgive, must find redress
in burning for ever the low flame
of his unquenchable bitterness.

Sic Itur ad Astra

Compared with these I am a saint,
  no judge would dare try me,
if the world wags on like this
  they will deify me.

July

Light and light and sunspots, fragrant colours,
in place of my heart *de rigeur*—bouquets.
Just this once, dear world, I will forgive you,
but from now on you'll have to mend your ways!

You sit and read

You sit and you read. How alone you are, even you don't know.
But sometimes you guess and then with a leisurely movement,
and a hint of mild animal sadness your simple features
dip into the light.

In front of the mirror

You take your face and slowly remove the paint,
but would remove the face that fate assigned you,
you wait for the armchair to rise and with a faint
gesture of boredom to appear behind you.

Contemplative

The old pose lost its charm. Let's take
a new one out. Yes, this will do.
In matters of dress it's all the same
what you fit your body to.
The dress, the body and the soul,
the same applies to everything.
When Thespis prinks, does she at all
suspect what change the colours bring?

Sincerity

Inspecting myself makes me bilious.
It's easier for the spontaneous.
I would if I could, be the driver of the dray
who washes great blonde horses all the day
and has nothing to say.

OXFORD POETS

Fleur Adcock
James Berry
Edward Kamau Brathwaite
Joseph Brodsky
Basil Bunting
W. H. Davies
Michael Donaghy
Keith Douglas
D. J. Enright
Roy Fisher
David Gascoyne
Ivor Gurney
David Harsent
Anthony Hecht
Zbigniew Herbert
Thomas Kinsella
Brad Leithauser
Derek Mahon
Medbh McGuckian
Jamie McKendrick
James Merrill
Peter Porter
Craig Raine
Christopher Reid
Stephen Romer
Carole Satyamurti
Peter Scupham
Penelope Shuttle
Louis Simpson
Anne Stevenson
George Szirtes
Grete Tartler
Edward Thomas
Charles Tomlinson
Chris Wallace-Crabbe
Hugo Williams